DINOSAUR WORLD
Double Bones
The Adventure of Diplodocus

Written by Michael Dahl

Illustrated by Garry Nichols

Special thanks to our advisers for their expertise:

Content Adviser: Philip J. Currie, Curator of Dinosaurs,
Royal Tyrrell Museum of Palaeontology, Drumheller, Alberta, Canada

Reading Adviser: Susan Kesselring, M.A., Literacy Educator,
Rosemount - Apple Valley - Eagan (Minnesota) School District

PICTURE WINDOW BOOKS
Minneapolis, Minnesota

Managing Editor: Catherine Neitge
Creative Director: Terri Foley
Art Director: Keith Griffin
Editor: Patricia Stockland
Designer: Joe Anderson
Page production: Picture Window Books
The illustrations in this book were prepared digitally.

Picture Window Books
5115 Excelsior Boulevard
Suite 232
Minneapolis, MN 55416
877-845-8392
www.picturewindowbooks.com

Printed in the United States of America.

Library of Congress Cataloging-in-Publication Data
Dahl, Michael.
Double bones : the adventure of Diplodocus / written by
Michael Dahl ; illustrated by Garry Nichols.
p. cm. — (Dinosaur world)
Includes bibliographical references and index.
ISBN 1-4048-0940-6 (hardcover)
1. Diplodocus—Pictorial works—Juvenile literature.
I. Nichols, Garry, 1958- ill. II. Title.

QE862.S3D28 2004
567.913—dc22   2004019920

No humans lived during the time of the dinosaurs. No person heard them roar, saw their scales, or felt their feathers.

The giant creatures are gone, but their fossils, or remains, lie hidden in the earth. Dinosaur skulls, skeletons, and eggs have been buried in rock for millions of years.

All around the world, scientists dig up fossils and carefully study them. Bones show how tall the dinosaurs stood. Claws and teeth show how they grabbed and what they ate. Scientists compare fossils with the bodies of living creatures such as birds and reptiles, which are relatives of the dinosaurs. Every year, scientists learn more and more about the giants that have disappeared.

Studying fossils and figuring out how the dinosaurs lived is like putting together the pieces of a puzzle that is millions of years old.

This is what some of those pieces can tell us about the dinosaur known as *Diplodocus* (di-PLOD-uh-kus).

A young *Diplodocus* opened its eyes and blinked. The morning sun was bright.

Diplodocus stretched its neck. The dinosaur looked around for its mother.

4

The mother *Diplodocus* was searching for food. She spied some tender leaves at the top of a tree.

The massive creature swung her long, powerful neck into the leaves. Chomp! Then she swept her head through the thick ferns at her feet.

Diplodocus is one of the longest dinosaurs that ever lived. An adult stretched 90 feet (27 meters) from its bony snout to the tip of its tail. *Diplodocus's* neck was as long as a school bus. Its whip-like tail could grow to 45 feet (13.5 m) in length. Fossils also show that *Diplodocus* had a row of spiny scales that looked like sharp teeth running along its back.

The young *Diplodocus* watched its mother. The adult dinosaur saw the leaves on the ground.

Diplodocus was an herbivore. It only ate plants. Its few teeth grew at the front of its mouth. The pencil-shaped teeth were good for ripping up leaves and twigs, but not for chewing. So, the dinosaur swallowed small stones along with the plants. The stones, called gastroliths, helped grind up the food inside the creature's stomach.

Both dinosaurs munched on the tasty leaves until the branches were bare, but they were soon hungry again.

The mother *Diplodocus* plodded heavily across the ground. She looked up and saw another tree with leaves at the very top.

This part of the forest was full of thick trees. *Diplodocus* had no room to swing her mighty neck. Instead, she reared up on her hind legs. She placed her thick front legs on a tree trunk and pushed it over. Crash!

Although *Diplodocus* had a long neck, it could not raise it very high. Some scientists think the dinosaur could lift its head up only 15 feet above the ground. *Diplodocus* was also too huge to enter some forests. Instead, it would poke its long neck between the trees and eat low-lying plants.

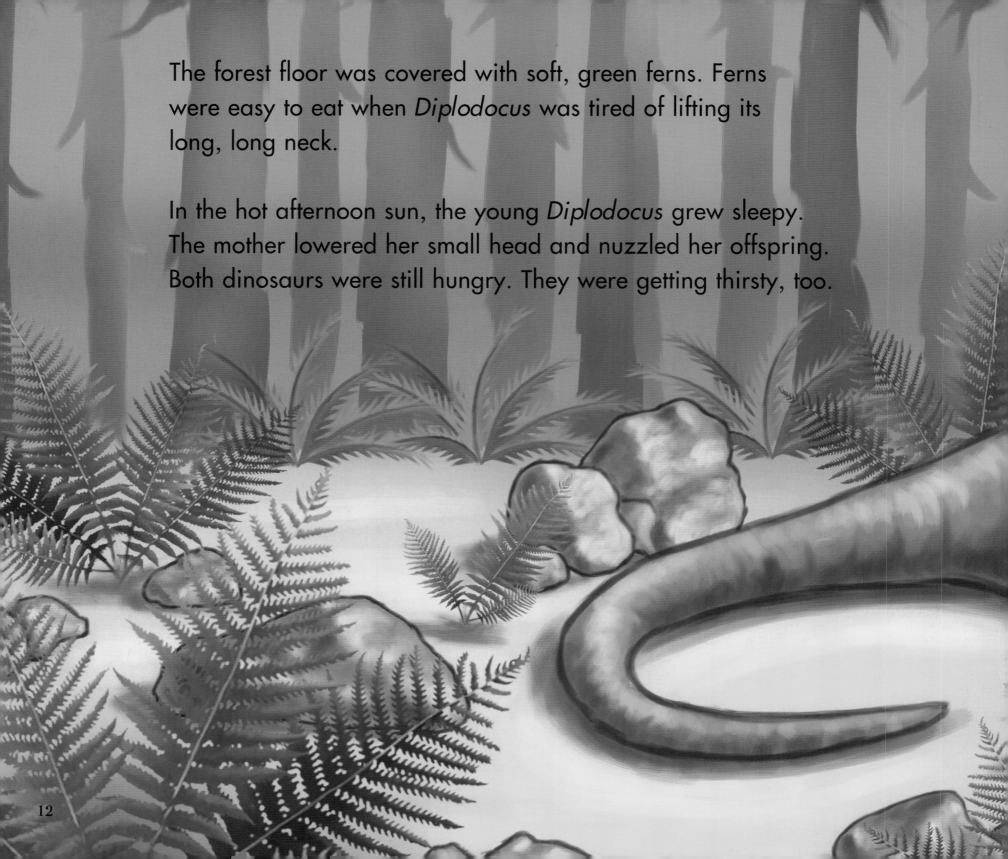

The forest floor was covered with soft, green ferns. Ferns were easy to eat when *Diplodocus* was tired of lifting its long, long neck.

In the hot afternoon sun, the young *Diplodocus* grew sleepy. The mother lowered her small head and nuzzled her offspring. Both dinosaurs were still hungry. They were getting thirsty, too.

Diplodocus mothers laid eggs. Some scientists think that the female dinosaur laid her eggs behind her as she walked along. Fossilized eggs have been found in long, straight lines. A few scientists believe *Diplodocus* mothers laid their eggs in nests on the ground and took care of their young.

The dinosaurs plodded slowly through the dim forest. At the edge of the trees, they found a wide lake. A light breeze blew over the waves. The water looked cool and refreshing.

The mother *Diplodocus* slowly climbed down the rocky slope. She stretched out her long, long neck toward the water. The young *Diplodocus* waited and watched.

Diplodocus means "double beam." Most dinosaurs had a single line of bones forming the neck. But in *Diplodocus*'s skeleton, the neck bones are divided into two rows, forming a single but powerful spine. Without this "double beam" of bones giving it extra support, *Diplodocus*'s neck would have been too long to move.

The young *Diplodocus* carefully crawled down the slope toward its mother. A few stones crunched beneath its elephant-like toes.

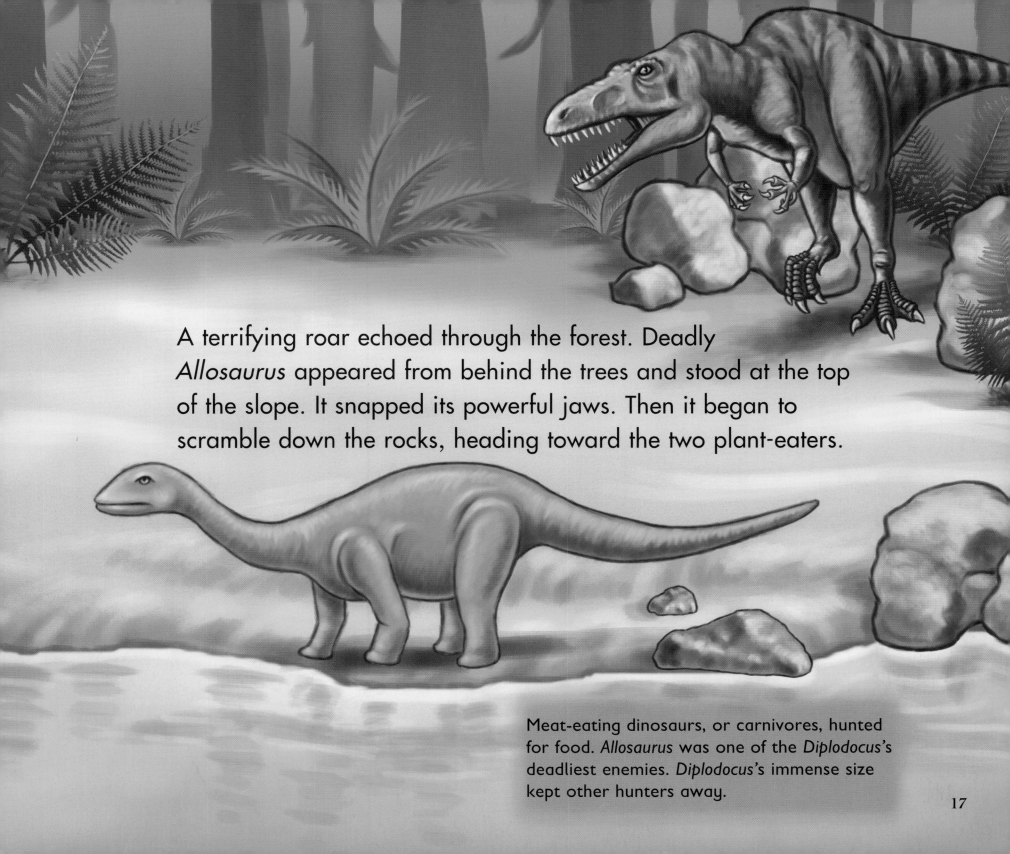

A terrifying roar echoed through the forest. Deadly *Allosaurus* appeared from behind the trees and stood at the top of the slope. It snapped its powerful jaws. Then it began to scramble down the rocks, heading toward the two plant-eaters.

Meat-eating dinosaurs, or carnivores, hunted for food. *Allosaurus* was one of the *Diplodocus*'s deadliest enemies. *Diplodocus*'s immense size kept other hunters away.

17

Mother and young both plunged into the lake. The grown *Diplodocus* used its front feet to touch the lake bottom. The younger dinosaur swam in the water alongside its mother.

Trackways are sets of dinosaur footprints left in mud or soft rock that have hardened over millions of years. Scientists study trackways to learn how dinosaurs moved. One trackway belonging to a *Diplodocus* shows only the front feet being used. Scientists believe this was made by the dinosaur as it traveled through deep water.

19

The young *Diplodocus* grew tired. It spent most of its time on dry land or in swampy fields. The dinosaur was growing weary from paddling through the deep water.

Diplodocus whipped its tail back and forth through the water, pushing its tired body forward. The other side of the lake grew closer and closer. The plant-eaters would soon be safe.

Scientists learn a lot about dinosaurs by studying modern-day animals. Elephants are some of the largest land animals that still survive on Earth. By watching how elephants move, live in herds, and take care of their young, scientists can guess how large dinosaurs like *Diplodocus* spent their time millions of years ago.

Diplodocus: Where ...

Diplodocus fossils have been discovered in the Rocky Mountain states of the western United States—western Colorado, Montana, Wyoming, and Utah.

... and When

The "Age of Dinosaurs" began 248 million years ago (mya). If we imagine the time from the beginning of the dinosaur age to the present as one day, the Age of Dinosaurs lasted 18 hours—and humans have only been around for 10 minutes!

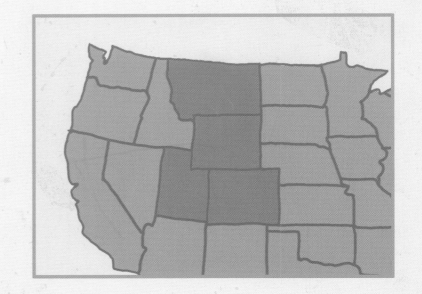

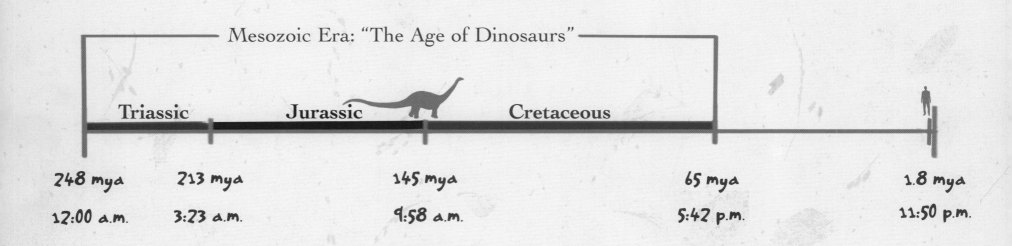

Mesozoic Era: "The Age of Dinosaurs"

| Triassic | Jurassic | Cretaceous | | |

| 248 mya | 213 mya | 145 mya | 65 mya | 1.8 mya |
| 12:00 a.m. | 3:23 a.m. | 9:58 a.m. | 5:42 p.m. | 11:50 p.m. |

Triassic—Dinosaurs first appear. Early mammals appear.
Jurassic—First birds appear.
Cretaceous—Flowering plants appear. By the end of this era, all dinosaurs disappear.

—First human appeared

—*Diplodocus* lived

Digging Deeper

Mighty Mowers

Diplodocus had one of the longest necks of any land animal on Earth. Scientists are still debating on how the dinosaur used its neck when eating. Most agree that *Diplodocus* kept its neck low most of the time. *Diplodocus* probably swung its long neck back and forth across the ground, eating moss, ferns, and shrubs. *Diplodocus* could have eaten up to half a ton of food in a day.

Whipper Snapper

Some scientists believed that *Diplodocus* could snap its long tail like a bullwhip. Computer models have shown that the dinosaur could lash its tail at a breath-taking speed of more than 740 miles per hour (331 meters per second). That's faster than the speed of sound! The loud whip-crack could have been used to scare away predators or to warn other dinosaurs of approaching danger.

Carnegie's Creatures

Andrew Carnegie was a wealthy American businessman who loved dinosaurs. During the late 1800s and early 1900s, he paid for many expeditions to hunt dinosaur fossils in the western United States. One of his teams in Wyoming discovered a complete *Diplodocus* skeleton. Carnegie ordered 11 reproductions to be made of the full-size fossil. Then he sent them to museums around the world. *Diplodocus*'s full name is *Diplodocus carnegii,* named after Andrew Carnegie.

Tail Fins

In 1990, a skin impression was found of a *Diplodocus*. The impression showed a row of boneless spines that traveled the length of the dinosaur's long back. The spines looked like teeth. The largest tooth-like spine sat near *Diplodocus*'s head and grew longer than a banana. Smaller spines covered the tip of the tail.

Words to Know

carnivore—a creature that only eats the meat of other living creatures

dinosaurs—giant creatures that lived millions of years ago; scientists think that many modern reptiles and birds are related to dinosaurs

gastrolith—stomach stones; rocks and pebbles inside a dinosaur's stomach help grind up its food

herbivore—a creature that eats only plants

impression—a mark or print made by pressing something down

predator—a creature that hunts other animals for food

spine—a sharp, stiff body part, or another name for a creature's backbone

trackway—a set of dinosaur footprints preserved in rock

To Learn More

At the Library
Cohen, Daniel. *Diplodocus*. Mankato, Minn.: Bridgestone Books, 2003.

Gray, Susan. *Diplodocus*. Chanhassen, Minn.: Child's World, 2004.

Matthews, Rupert. *Diplodocus*. Chicago: Heinemann Library, 2003

On the Web
FactHound offers a safe, fun way to find Web sites related to this book. All of the sites on FactHound have been researched by our staff. *www.facthound.com*

1. Visit the FactHound home page.
2. Enter a search word related to this book, or type in this special code: 1404809406
3. Click on the FETCH IT button.

Your trusty FactHound will fetch the best Web sites for you!

Index